SALES

—It's That Simple

SALES

—It's That Simple

The 8 Principles of Sales

Dave Slain

Sales—It's That Simple: The 8 Principles of Sales

Copyright © 2008 Dave Slain. All rights reserved. No part of this book may be reproduced or retransmitted in any form or by any means without the written permission of the publisher.

Published by Wheatmark®
610 East Delano Street, Suite 104
Tucson, Arizona 85705 U.S.A.
www.wheatmark.com

International Standard Book Number: 978-1-58736-901-8
Library of Congress Control Number: 2007930449

Contents

About the Author 7
Acknowledgments 9

Introduction 11
The Eight Simple Principles of Sales 21
#1: Think Positively 27
#2: Form a Defined Strategy 39
#3: Know Your Product 49
#4: Resolve 53
#5: Have the Ability to Change 61
#6: Execute 67
#7: Ask 73
#8: Understand the Differential Theory 77
Conclusion 87

About the Author

So, why did I write this book? It's simple: to positively influence people's lives. I firmly believe that my techniques will work for anyone in any industry. In sales, many people work too hard and allow the negative aspects of life to dominate their existence. I would like to generate a more positive feeling about sales and show people that even a slight change in their method of thinking will result in significant improvements in their selling success.

I am like you: a sales or business professional who works hard to compete in today's business world. The only difference is that I've taken the time to study the aspects of sales that make a difference, and I've been able to effectively implement these techniques and devise a plan to improve one's sales performance. It's worth pointing out that I am still actively working in the field I'm writing about.

Dave Slain

I graduated from college in 1994 with a major in communications and concentrations in advertising and public relations. I wanted to be a radio DJ or possibly a TV producer. However, after I graduated I found that my best opportunity was in the field of sales. This opportunity came to me by chance and not by design, but I embraced my challenge and began to learn how to effectively sell. I've been selling for over thirteen years now with tremendous success. I've achieved this success by studying what works and doesn't work in today's business world. Who would have imagined that in thirteen short years I would be the vice president of sales and marketing, leading the growth and profit charge of a small company—a charge that is well on its way to double the size of the company in 5 short years. I accomplished this growth by teaching my strategies to my sales department, who had the belief and discipline to execute those strategies.

Lastly, let me point out that I do not have a degree in human behavior or psychology. The opinions I share in this book are based on my experiences within sales and life in general.

Acknowledgments

This book is the result of information gathered from many sources. It includes understanding gained from books, lectures, seminars, and my own work experience. It also comes from training I've received from individuals who have given me insight into a better way to sell (and in some cases, a better way to live). The sheer number of these people prevents me from thanking each one individually here; however, all of you who have been a major part of my professional career know who you are. Thanks to each of you, and thanks to all of you who have put out books, seminars, and lectures that have helped educate me about better selling techniques.

I would also like to thank my mom and dad for always believing in me and supporting each and every move I've made. My parents always instilled in me the belief that I could do whatever I wanted to do. They taught me that anything is possible, and I'm very grateful that they did. Finally, I would like to thank my brothers, sisters, grandparents, and close friends for being a supporting part of my life. I know that I can always count on you, and that deserves a "thank-you" that lasts forever.

Special thanks to Steve Hammond, who was the first person to introduce me to the field of sales. I personally owe this man more than he will ever know for building my foundation and starting me on the path to success. I cannot express my gratitude in words, but he has my utmost respect and admiration.

Special thanks to Jackie Kuehlmann-Skroch for all your help in making this book a reality.

Introduction

We live in a competitive world, and the strain of being in sales is incredibly demanding. Each and every day we have to be at our best. If we aren't, we can lose what we've worked so hard to build. My mission is to know that people are benefiting from my book and improving their sales performances, whether they are experienced professionals or just starting sales careers.

Selling is sometimes perceived as one of the most difficult and feared jobs out there today. After all, sales often involves public speaking, a common fear for most of us. In my opinion, the negative perception of sales is mostly due to the fear of rejection. Sales is also feared because one runs the risk of sounding like an idiot; clear communication is required. Fear of rejection by itself makes the actual simplicity of selling challenging to understand.

In addition, sales is often viewed as a sleazy profession that forces people to push products onto friends and relatives. It is also commonly believed that salespeople like to use manipulative data and fancy talk that make the purchasing experience more difficult for the buyer.

Both friends and customers have told me that they do not trust what they have heard from someone working in sales. These educated, professional people had a hard time believing what they heard because it came from a salesperson. People remember what I call the "old-school sales" of telling them anything they want to hear in order to get them to buy, and as such customers perceive the sales industry with specific stereotypes. Trust is a large concern and will be for quite some time. Not everyone is going to be honest, and that will keep this perception alive; however, you can overcome it by following the principles set forth in this book.

Furthermore, consider the general perception of salespeople. Why would a car dealership advertise that it has no salespeople or that it does not pay commission? The answer is easy: the general public does not have a rosy view of sales or those who have made it their career. Obviously, the dealerships *wants* people to buy vehicles; that is why it exists. The bottom line is that having no salespeople is an advertising ploy designed to entice buyers to show up at the dealership, whereupon they will receive a different, less conventional type of sale. Since there are allegedly "no salespeople," the consumer is less defensive and more likely to listen to the features and benefits as truths instead of the salesperson's opinion or manipulative spin.

The point? Due to the perceived reputation of the sales profession, it is inherently difficult to become a *great* salesperson. If you're not convinced of this, ask yourself how many truly effective salespeople are out there. How many people can deliver results year-in and year-out? Not many—and those who do are working really hard and probably sacrificing their personal lives as a result. Sales in itself does not have to be a complicated, mixed portfolio of charts and diagrams about how to grow business. In fact, to be great, you just need a simple method of sales.

Here are some common questions that sales professionals all ask ourselves. These questions—and how you react when you ask them—are of vital importance.

- Why can I not close that account?

- I know my product is the best in the marketplace. Why can't they see that?

- It's not fair—he doesn't work that much, but he always get more business than I do. Why is that?

- How can I reach that goal?

- Why do the goals set by the company seem unachievable?

- Why does my boss always set me up for failure?

- Why do bad things happen to me?

- Why is my prospect list more difficult to close than the lists of the other reps?

- Why haven't I earned that business yet?

- Why doesn't someone just help me?

- How come my customers just don't make sense?

- My customers do not understand what is good for them. Why do they continually screw themselves up?

- Why should I have to give up my personal time?

Most of the time, we ask these questions because we feel selfish or have negative attitudes. Being selfish is not uncommon in today's society. Selfishness leads to a feeling of helplessness, and it prevents us from fully seeing and understanding all the available options. Asking ourselves these questions normally indicates that we do not believe in ourselves.

Although this book is not about society, I feel the need to make one major point. In modern times, we have become partially an "all about me" society; that is, people tend to focus on themselves and their beliefs. In itself, this is not a bad thing. We all need to take care of ourselves and continue to better our understandings and beliefs. We all need to work to improve ourselves, yet for some reason a lot of us feel that if we hold certain opinions, then we have to convince everyone else to share these opinions. We don't try to understand why our peers have different beliefs. In some cases, we are so opinionated that we isolate and/or humiliate ourselves or others.

Having opinions is a wonderful thing; everyone should have his or her own beliefs. As salespeople, however, we must be willing to understand other people's thought processes. We cannot be selfish. We need to concentrate on our families, our company, and our customers. Do not confuse selfishness in any way with goal setting and the desire to make a better life for yourself. That is not being selfish; it is just being goal-oriented.

Earlier in my career, I had a prospective account in San Francisco. I continued to call on them on a weekly, sometimes daily, basis. I put in hundreds of hours to get this account, but over and over again I was denied. Finally, after a year of trying to get in contact with them, I received a return call—*a return call!* I remember thinking *Yes, this is a glorious day. Nothing can stop me now.* I went in to the account and gave a great presentation—so good that the prospect immediately asked me to supply a pricing–and–conversion strategy.

I was called into the prospect's office to review my proposal for their business. They liked everything but my pricing, which they said was 20 percent high.

At that time in my career, my thought process was: *It's not my fault. I've done all I can, and if my company cannot be competitive, there is nothing I can do about it.* To make matters worse, my company told me that I still needed to hit my target sales number, regardless of anything else. I remember telling my sales manager, "I brought the business to you, but you couldn't get it." He agreed but said that was not how the business world worked.

Who was right—me or the company? At the time, I thought I was right. However, the fact of the matter is that I was dead wrong. I was being selfish. I had an attitude that *It's not my problem; it's someone else's fault.* As soon as you have selfish thoughts like this, you stop learning and either slow down or lose some of your sales effectiveness. The right answer is that it is always your problem, and it is always within your control.

Back to the questions listed previously. Can you stop yourself from asking those questions? Maybe, maybe not. What's important is what you do with yourself if you ask these questions. You need to understand the difference between when you are selfish and when you are unselfish. A selfish response is usually negative, such as believing the problem is someone else's fault. An unselfish response usually results in you finding a better or more effective way to accomplish the goal or task at hand.

All of this is linked to one key factor: *we all think differently.* What else can explain why people can attend the same meeting and then interpret it in different ways? It's because we do not all think alike. (I will be repeating this point many times.) You and several others may hear a story together, but how many will repeat the facts and details in exactly the same way? Not very many. Why? The answer is simple: we all think differently.

I know that right now there are people thinking *Wait a minute. I know a lot of people who think like me.* Do you really? Or are you simply telling people your opinion, and they aren't responding? Could it be that people are just agreeing with you because they don't want to argue and debate? What is the real answer?

Earl Nightingale (1921–1989), who was known as the greatest philosopher of his time, recorded over seven thousand radio programs and wrote multiple inspirational and motivational books over the course of his career. Earl once said, "You become what you think about." I find great truth in this statement. Think about it. How many people do you know who worry all the time? They are nervous wrecks. Why? They simply became what they thought about. As each of us grew up, we developed into what we are today. Our general views are different. Our hobbies are different. Our taste in women or men is different. What we like to do for fun is different. Whether you realize it or not, we all have many differences; this in itself is natural.

What fun would our lives be if everyone was the same? Our individual points of difference are directly related to why each of us acts differently in any given situation. In some cases, we realize that we're different and then try to convert others to be more like us. Maybe you've had a friend or family member who was in trouble and you couldn't understand how he or she got into that situation. Then you lectured the person and told him how he needed to change his life. In short, you gave him the best lecture you could think of because you loved him. A short period of time passed, and trouble again became the person's middle name. Then you were *really* upset with him. *Why didn't he listen to me?* you thought. *I just don't understand.* Now, think about that last statement: *I just do not understand.* Remember, we all think differently. We may not understand each other because we continue to get lost in our own thoughts and opinions rather than listening to others and understanding why they think the way they do.

Sales is more about people than anything else. It's about effective communication and your ability to convince another person to make a purchase. You do this by paying attention to the often overlooked key points of sales—things like how you think while you're selling and what you think while you're developing your plan and exploring your product options. Sales is about what others want to know rather than what you want to tell them. Start paying attention to how others think and what they want rather than simply telling them what you think. Thus, the eight principles are born: to teach you to become an effective salesperson within any market or condition.

The Eight Simple Principles of Sales

When people talk about a key principle of sales, it sounds so simple and easy. It *is* simple, but it's not easy. Each of you needs to decide to take the time to learn and understand these principles. When I was initially writing this book, I gave a copy of the first draft to one of my sales representatives. He, on his own, wrote them on his whiteboard and spent time practicing the principles. I noticed that he had them up there for a year. At the end of the year, he received the single largest check he had ever received. The *principles* work, but do *you* want to?

I've created eight simple principles of sales, some of which may not be new to you. It is important to note that the major differences I will teach you will explain what actions you must take within each strategy and what order you should learn each strategy to maximize your future success. A key element of making these principles work is following them in the order that they are written. Start with number one, and end with number eight. Once you fully understand one principle, move on to the next. The eight simple principles of sales are as follows:

1. Think Positively

2. Form a Defined Strategy

3. Know Your Product

4. Resolve

5. Have the Ability to Change

6. Execute

7. Ask

8. Understand the Diffcrential Theory

Each principle feeds off the other. As you work through each principle, you will be introduced to the next level; hence, the order of the principles is crucial. Positive thinking is the beginning of the beginning. Without positive thinking, the power of negativity will cause the rest of the principles to fail. Thinking positively (1) about what you are doing and why you are doing it can, by itself, allow you to put together a successful, clearly defined strategy (2) for achieving success in your field. Once you develop that strategy, you can understand your product (3) at the level you need to in order to fully explain your product to the potential customer. As time progresses, more positive thoughts will enter your mind and allow you to build effective strategies, all of which will propel you into a new level of consistency, which in this book is called resolve (4).

Once you understand resolve, you will begin to realize what specific steps you need to take to become better at what you do—in other words, you will gain the ability to change (5). With principle 6, execute, you will learn to convert each principle to action steps within your skill set. Once you have understood and applied principles 1 through 5, then you need to determine whether you have fully executed the proper improvements and asked the correct questions (7).

The final principle is designed to move you into a new level of effective selling. Understanding the differential theory, however, will be at its highest level of effectiveness only if you have understood and applied principles one through seven first.

I recommend that you read this book cover to cover and then go back through each principle and learn them in order. In the course of learning each principle, you will begin to see their connections with each other and why the order is important. Do not change the order of understanding, and do not assume that you have understood a principle without first making that principle a part of your everyday life. These may be simple principles, but the challenge lies in understanding them. Are you ready to accept that challenge? Then let's proceed.

The Eight Principles Feed Off Each Other:

It starts with **Thinking Positively.**
Then you can **Form a Defined Strategy,**
Which will show you how to **Know Your Product,**
Which will help you get the **Resolve,**
Which will teach you how to **Have the Ability to Change,**
Which will let you **Execute** your improvements,
Which will allow you to **Ask** for the sale in an effective manner.

Finally, to be really great, you need to **Understand the Differential Theory,** which you can only truly accomplish once you complete the first seven principles.

#1

Think Positively

You have heard this before. The difference? This time *you need to listen*. Your thought process will determine your success. Changing your thoughts to only positive ones alone will show tremendous results. This is a negative world. You just need to read the newspaper or watch the news to see all of the bad things happening around us. I would guess that the bad-to-good ratio of events reported in the media is 10:1—ten negative or "bad" reports to one "good" or positive report.

We are programmed to think negatively. Overcoming this is a challenging task, but I'm going to show you how to do it. Understand that banishing negative thoughts is a constant battle, one that will never go away. The way to overcome negativity is to be aware of when you are negative.

We often don't know when or why we are being negative, so how can we overcome it? Here is the secret: every morning, wake up and tell yourself, *I am going to be positive today. Today is a great day!* I'm serious. Do this exercise each and every morning, and you'll start to catch your own negativity. If every morning you tell yourself that you will be positive, then being positive will become automatic. At the very least, you will catch yourself when you're being negative. After a while, that ability will become second nature. Once you identify when you are negative, you can correct those negative thoughts by converting them into positive thoughts.

That is an important step that bears repeating: once you catch yourself being negative, you must convert those negative comments or thoughts into positive comments or thoughts. Pay attention, now—I said *comment or thought*. Yes, even if you only *think* something negative, you must convert it into something positive. Our thoughts are often more powerful than the words we speak. We internalize our thoughts, and they can eat at us. Make sure that you correct your negative thoughts.

Here is a real-life example of how to turn a negative thought into a positive thought. I had one of our accounts call and notify us that the director of procurement was being let go. Not only was this individual skilled at her job, she was also an ally of our company and fully understood the benefits we brought to the table. My sales rep's first thought—and one I might have easily shared—was *Oh, no—we're going to lose the account.*

However, instead of giving in to negative thinking, my thoughts were immediately to help the director of procurement find another job. Helping people you work with find new jobs in times of turmoil is just as important as supporting them while they are gainfully employed. Either way, you should treat your buyers as you would want to be treated and assist them like you would any other friend. I also viewed this situation as an opportunity to get to know more people within our current customers organization and to strengthen our relationship with them. At the time, I had no idea what would happen, but I can guarantee that if I had thought negatively, we would have lost the account. As it turned out, this account is under new management today and we continue to build our relationship together.

Being positive creates a sense of confidence that others can't help but notice. People want to listen to us if we're positive. Everyone wants to be part of a positive experience, and people will flock to you as you perfect the power of thinking positively.

Another example of positive thinking is when I was notified by a very large account that we would be losing $8 million of business. Devastating news! How could we continue to exist? To make matters worse, I had been on the job for only six months. How could we recover—myself *and* the company as a whole? Yes, those thoughts crossed my mind.

Even with the $8 million loss, this account would remain one of our top five accounts, however, it was a very unpleasant experience for everyone at my company. We didn't lose the account on price, service, or quality. We were a preferred supplier and lost the account due to an internal decision to move to a substrate we could not produce. Even though it was a difficult time, I practiced my own methods and always reversed my negative comments and thoughts.

How did I do that? Actually, it was quite simple. The account had inadvertently caused us to become stagnant. Instead of focusing on the negative, I looked at this situation as an opportunity to set new goals, enter into new markets, and re-create a new sales strategy. I developed this plan with the idea that in the long run, we would be a better, stronger company and that we *would* get those sales dollars back.

I delivered a strong message to my sales force that explained to each of them that we could recover from such a major loss. In addition, I introduced a growth plan and initiative to illustrate that we would be around for the long-term. In the end, we lost $8 million worth of sales, but we sold an additional $11 million that year and finished $3 million dollars ahead of the previous year. Not only did we more than recover, we ended up with a sales engine that is continuing to show growth today. Most likely, none of that would have happened if we had folded to negativity under the pressure of such devastating news.

A positive thought process doesn't just apply to major disasters, however; it also applies to the little things. Try not to be critical of others, such as when starting sentences with the word *why*: *Why does he always do that? Why can't she just leave me alone? Why should I have to do that—it's his job? Why? Why? Why?*

When being critical of others, think of the word *why* as negative. When trying to understand someone or something, think of the word *why* as positive. If you catch yourself being critical of others, stop immediately and rethink what you're going to say. Instead of asking, *Why should I have to do that?* ask yourself instead, *What can I do to help this person understand what I'm asking him or her to do?* Or *How can I help this person understand that he or she can help me get the right answer for this situation?* During the course of a day, you may catch yourself saying, *Why did this happen to me?* Change that comment to *How can I learn from this?*

Let's look at the power of positive thinking and how your thinking can affect your life. Remember the earlier quote, *You become what you think about.* That in itself is the secret to understanding this principle. If you continually complain at work, guess what will happen? You will continue to find things to complain about.

Let's say things aren't going well for you, and you're always thinking *poor me*. Whether we realize it or not, our thoughts directly control our actions. If you're always looking for things that are wrong or unfair, you will always find things that are wrong and unfair. If you never think you can succeed, you will probably not succeed.

If you always say you have no time, you will not have any time. I personally constantly struggle to think positively about time. You may wonder how it is negative to say that you have no time. It isn't negative per se, but it does make my point: your thoughts can become your reality. Because I tell myself I have no time, I have no time. When I tell myself I *do* have time to get everything done, amazingly enough I normally get it all done.

Our thoughts control what we do; if we think positively, we will automatically bring positive results to ourselves. Does this mean that nothing bad or negative will ever come into your life? Of course not—

positive and negative acts happen all the time. It's how you *react* to events, though, that will determine your future. If a negative event occurs and you only think negatively about it, then *more* negative things will likely happen. Conversely, if a negative event occurs and you remain positive in attitude, then in most cases a more positive, enjoyable life will eventually come your way. And if you are able to stay positive, good things will always be around the corner—even if they're hidden among some negatives. The worst-case scenario of positive thinking is that you reduce your personal amount of negativity and live a happier and healthier life.

Thinking positively is not difficult to do; rather, it is difficult to maintain. This is where we, as ordinary people, tend to fall short. Maintaining positive thinking is difficult because of all the negativity we live in. Our friends and colleagues will normally offer little or no help. Those closest to us will often bring us down with their own doubt and negativity. They don't realize that they're dragging us down and may, in fact, think they're helping us. They just do not realize they are being negative, and furthermore they do not realize what effect they can have on us.

For example, let's say you want to take a new job in a different industry. You are excited and feel ready for this great opportunity. As you tell your family and friends, you begin to hear things like, "Why are you taking such a big risk? You know nothing about that industry. You'd be starting over." All that you hear is "concern" for you and your future. The result? You begin to doubt the decision you made. Such doubt can lead to even more negative thoughts, which will eventually impact your performance; ultimately, things will likely not work out.

So what do you do? Isolate yourself from those you care most about? Absolutely not! What you do is concentrate each and every night on positive thoughts. As you go through the day, ask questions that begin with *what* and *how*: *What can I do to make my dream come true? How can I better impact my sales results?* End the day with positive thoughts, and start the day with positive thoughts. As you go through your day, catch your negative thoughts and think how you can turn them into something positive.

I can already hear one statement that many of you may be thinking as you read this section: being negative and facing reality are not the same things. In most cases, I don't agree. If you ever hear yourself say, "That's just how it is," then you are thinking negatively.

Can you change a result that has already happened? In business, yes, you can change the result. Although you may not have an immediate opportunity, you can always affect the impact and change the result. Let's say you lose an account or get shoved aside in a customer bid. If you think *Well, that's over,* you are not thinking positively. Instead, think of what you can do to improve or how you can overcome any obstacles. Do not ever concentrate on the negativity that has been brought about by negative results. Instead, immediately believe that you can overcome the challenge that has just been put in front of you.

A perfect example of this is when I talked about my old company's prices being 20 percent too high in the introduction section of this book. My immediate thoughts were that it wasn't my fault and there was nothing I could do about it. According to my job description, that was true; as a sales professional, however, it was not. Because I concentrated on the fact that there was nothing that I could do, I did nothing but complain. That didn't help anyone. In fact, it hurt me in the long run because I could have been learning instead of complaining.

Now when I deal with similar pricing challenges, I research what *really* happened: *Was my comparison "apples to apples"? What production process did we and our competitor use? Can we run it differently? What is the financial situation of the company who was awarded the business? What other material may work that we have not already thought of?* The list goes on. In today's environment, when I face pricing issues, I can make an informed decision: *Am I better off concentrat-*

ing elsewhere, or do I need to continue to go after this account? Unless you spend time figuring out what went wrong, while at the same time staying positive, you will encounter the same unwanted results in a similar situation in the future.

I can't understand how each of you thinks because *we all think differently.* Therefore, I can't use examples that will apply to everyone. Your challenge will be to catch yourself when you are negative and turn your situation into a positive. It can be done, but you must make a conscious effort. Remember my secret: wake up every morning, and tell yourself that you will be positive. Tell yourself that today is going to be a great day. Do it—it works!

Positive thinking is not arrogance or thinking that you are better than someone else. It is also not being trapped in a false reality. A great example is the people trying out for *American Idol*. Some can really sing, and some ... oh my. Yet all of them *think* they are good. Those who think they're good but are in fact terrible are caught in a false reality. If you're not growing your business or your business is slowly slipping away, you shouldn't believe that you are an awesome salesperson. Conversely, if you land a big account through minimal effort, don't fall into the trap of thinking that the results were all you. A false reality will lead you down a path of exhaustive failure. Each of us needs to be able to do a reality check.

It is difficult to know how good you really are until you can do an effective self-evaluation. To honestly evaluate yourself, you need to dig deep inside and face the truth—not something you've convinced yourself of. Be careful of those false realities, as they are not always easy to recognize. Practicing the eight principles will make you more readily able to evaluate yourself. Begin with positive thinking. Once that has become a part of your daily life, move on to principle 2: forming a defined strategy.

#1 Think Positively
Focus Points:

You've heard it before, but **LISTEN THIS TIME.**
You think this is silly. **MAYBE, BUT IT WORKS.**
You always skip this part; **DON'T.**
You don't believe in it? **START BELIEVING!**

How to Think Positively
Be aware of when you are negative; only then can you overcome it.
Correct it immediately by replacing the negative thought with a positive thought.
Tell yourself every morning: *I am going to be positive, and today is going to be a great day.*

The Power of Thinking Positively
Will catapult you to a new level in life
Will change your daily view
Will make you happier
Will make you more successful
Will help you achieve your goals
Will create more opportunities in your life
Will set you free

Positive = Power

#2

Form a Defined Strategy

Blindly going into a sales call will more often than not lead to failure, just as blindly calling on anything or anyone without a defined strategy will lead to failure. This principle is an overlooked and complicated part of sales. Those who use it tend to complicate it. Others skip it because it can be challenging to think about.

Fear not. Because you are always to stay positive, I have a simple solution. A defined strategy does not necessarily mean a detailed fifty-page report with charts and graphs illustrating your thought process and reasons for movement. In fact, I would recommend against that. A large report will lose you in the details rather then allowing you to spend time on what matters most: what the customer wants. I've written this chapter specifically for the salespeople and not the managers. Managers need to follow a slightly different path. If you would like more information on how managers need to better define a strategy, go to the website I've developed to help all salespeople improve their skills and gain a better understanding of their capabilities: www.sales-itworks.com.

Now back to salespeople and how to properly define your strategy. On a sheet of paper, write the details that give you the confidence to talk with your prospect or customer. The simple fact that you wrote down those points will benefit you more than you realize.

Write down the facts that are most important to you—those that make you most prepared and thus give you the most confidence. A gentleman I work with needs to research a prospective company on the Internet and understand the latest business movements. He feels the need to comment to the buyer on the latest news because he likes to show that he understands their business. This arms him with the confidence he needs to get and keep the customer's attention.

Once you reach the level of confidence that you feel is necessary to be prepared to do sales, you need to conduct enough research to compile a list of questions for the customer. Write these questions in a way that will lead to the answers you are looking for. Your goal should be to get prospects to talk as much as possible and teach you about their business. Conversely, when it is time, you should be teaching *them* about *your* business.

Let's summarize this into a simple formula to follow. Again, it is important to tailor the questions to you and your own personality. So, list the questions that fit your personality and give you the confidence you need to pursue that account. Your list should enable you to do the following:

1. Identify the product base.

2. Relate to the buyer.

3. Ask about the current supplier.

4. Ask about innovation.

5. Discuss cost savings.

At what point in the conversation do you do that? Let's look at an example. At a large, European-based account, here were my questions (asked via phone):

1. What are your major growth products?

2. What do you need to help take cost out of your main (replace with answer to question 1) product(s)?

3. Do you have any problems with your current supplier? What are those problems, and how do you think they should be resolved?

4. Is your company interested in innovation?

5. What type of innovation interests you?

6. Does your current supply base offer you cost-savings proposals?

Those were my questions. Simple, huh? Some people might be analyzing those questions, believing that one should always ask open-ended questions or disbelieving that those types of questions work. Well, I am here to tell you that they *did* work. They worked because I was prepared and because I asked the questions that allowed me to effectively communicate with complete confidence. The questions need to fit your personality so that a dialogue can begin with your prospect. Again, this section is about your confidence. Let's look a little deeper into why these questions worked.

- I asked about the company's product, thus asking about their business.

- I asked about the purchasing agent's job, thus making it relevant to them on an individual basis.

- I asked about their supply situation because we all need to know whether the current supplier is liked.

- I asked about innovation to help lead the buyer into telling me what key areas they are concentrating on, so I know how to talk about innovation with them.

- I asked more about innovation in case they gave a simple answer like "yes."

- I asked about cost savings from my competitors to find out if this could be a point of difference. Many suppliers overlook cost savings with current accounts.

You can have as many questions as you would like, but remember: it is a dialogue and discussion; do not get lost or stuck in the questions. Concentrate on understanding the answers to the questions. Do not read the questions. Rather, *ask* the questions, as in normal conversation. I would recommend writing the questions on a sheet of paper and then throwing it out prior to the meeting. Or, just summarize the questions on a notepad that you can quickly reference to ensure that you don't forget anything important. Throwing out your list or writing a summary will force you to engage in conversation with your clients rather than reading questions. If you read a question rather than ask it, you will lose the personal touch of a normal conversation, which risks isolating the buyer. Furthermore, you will likely hurry through your list of questions rather than paying attention to the answers and properly exploring the first question.

I could go on and on in this category because there are so many pitfalls. Just remember: keeping it simple is the key to an effective defined strategy.

Now that we've established that a defined strategy is about confidence and that you need to keep things simple, we need to discuss the *listening* part of sales. You are asking these questions for a reason, so pay attention to the answers. Often we get so excited about our message that our minds race to what we're going to say next and we forget to listen. Oh, we shake our heads and act like we understand the message, but in the end we just keep blabbering about what we want to say. Unfortunately, we just skipped over the most important message like a burnt piece of toast. Why? Because salespeople forget to listen.

In fact, most people forget to listen. It's not actually difficult to listen; we just don't do it. Why is that? Let's get back to confidence. Arming ourselves with confidence through preparation will allow us to have good conversations with our clients. Lack of confidence will lead us to just keep talking; after all, if the client brings up something we don't know about, it might ruin the sale … right? Now that's negative thinking. In reality, the opposite is true. If you're unsure about something, today's buyers will respect an answer of "I'll get back to you on that." Just make sure that you do, indeed, get back to them—and quickly.

I can remember a sales call that went bad because I didn't listen to what my customer was telling me. The customer was a large candy company, and my company at the time had a small percentage of the business. At my first meeting with the buyer, I was so busy talking or thinking about what I was going to say next that I didn't listen to what she was saying. In fact, my follow-up list didn't even mention the "real" opportunity.

During the course of the meeting, the buyer mentioned that the primary vendor was having quality issues. My eyes got big and I thought, *Oh yeah, this is my chance.* My buyer went on to say the problem was that they were not willing to pay more for their product. She then noted that they were also introducing new products within this category, and sales were expected to grow substantially.

Here's what I wrote in my follow-up notes: *having quality issues, but not willing to pay more.* Is that what you would have written? Why did I not listen? The answer is simple: I didn't listen because I lacked a defined strategy. I didn't do the proper research that would have enabled me to accurately market my product. Because I didn't have a defined strategy, I lacked the confidence to manage the issues that were brought up during the meeting.

In this example, what should I have done? The answers are endless; there is no single "right" answer. The wrong answer is to do just what I did, which was nothing. One possible strategy would have been to further investigate the quality issue and find out what was causing the client concerns in this area. I could have asked how the client measured cost—simply by the per-thousand price of the raw good? The list goes on. If I would have been more prepared and had a defined strategy, I could have closed the gap and positioned my company for a sale.

Issues, however, are great talking points during a meeting because that is when the salesperson has the opportunity to address concerns and fallacies. Never be afraid to address issues or problems; instead, embrace them as the opportunities that they are. Never think of issues as being "bad." Rather, recognize that an issue is the one chance to set the record straight or to understand the key points that your customers want and need. Now that you understand (or your customer understands), you are further along on your way to a sale.

Sales—It's That Simple

The best strategy is to have the confidence that results from adequate preparation. If you prepare well and feel confident, you will find a better way to present to your clients. Presentations evolve into conversations, which then evolve into sales. Conversations are two-way speaking engagements. If you talk a lot more than your customer, you aren't listening enough. Confidence, through proper preparation, allows us everything we need to get us going down the path to effective communication with our customers. A defined strategy in your own terms will deliver that confidence and force you to think through your strategy, thus giving you more confidence. Thought is the key to confidence. This principle forces you to give thought to each important aspect involved in gaining confidence. Pretty cool, isn't it?

Now, as you improve on defining your strategy, you will notice that it doesn't take much time. You will soon be able to define your strategy and be ready for a meeting in a short period of time. Keep working on this principle, and once you feel that it's part of your daily life, move on to principle 3: know your product.

#2 Form a Defined Strategy Focus Points:

A defined strategy is the "how to" portion of sales.

It is:
Overlooked
Skipped
Complicated

It is *not*:
A fifty-page report with graphs and charts
The same for everyone
The mindset of *You are right and I am wrong*

The Secrets of a Defined Strategy:
Write down your thoughts before the meeting. List your questions on paper. Don't have the questions or notes in front of you; simply have topics for discussion.

A Defined Strategy = Confidence!

#3

Know Your Product

Enough said. I won't spend a lot of time on this point, as it is something you already know you need to do. If you don't know your product, your customers will be able to tell almost immediately. Buyers today are very sharp and very busy. They don't have time for people who cannot help them perform better. Now more than ever, you must know your product. If you are new to sales or even a seasoned professional, never act like you know your product if you really don't. Be honest.

I can remember when I first started out in sales. I would try and fake my knowledge of the product during initial presentations. If you are new to the field, don't make this mistake. There are a few reasons why honesty is the best policy. Buyers are very sharp; they understand what they buy and what key components make up their purchase. They also have many contacts within the industry; they can call and ask their contact questions and get quick accurate answers regarding the product you are trying to sell. Always give your buyers credit and assume that they may know more than you.

I have heard many unique (and often inventive) arguments from different salespeople on why product knowledge doesn't matter. One of my good friends—let's call him Mike—is a great salesman. Mike always tells me that he does not need to know about the product to sell it. Although that is what he believes, he certainly doesn't follow his own advice, as he can tell you more about the products he sells than almost anyone else. Whether he realizes it or not, that product knowledge is what helps set him apart from his competition. Although he thinks he doesn't need it, he certainly studies the products he sells and continues to thrive. All great sales people know their products well.

While I agree that product knowledge is not what gives you the skill to sell, it *does* give you the confidence and understanding that enables you to have a suitable conversation with your client. If you don't understand the basic features and benefits of your product, or the key production points, you're putting yourself at a major disadvantage to the competition. If a buyer starts to ask you questions, and you do not know the answers, you can either deflect and change the subject or make something up. Contrarily, if you know the answer and can further explain the benefits of your product, you have automatically set yourself apart from many other sales individuals, and hopefully you have begun to gain their confidence.

Remember principle 2: form a defined strategy? Principles 2 and 3 work hand in hand to build confidence. People forget that success is based on confidence—not arrogance, but confidence in what you do and how you do it. How do you get that confidence? Simple—you properly prepare and define your plan, and you understand your product. Then you will have the necessary confidence. Being a sales individual does not preclude you from being knowledgeable about your products. Instead, it is a necessity that you must embrace; without it you will never be effective on a long-term or repeat basis.

#3 Know Your Product Focus Points:

Never fake it.
Always be honest.
You don't have to be an expert—but it helps.
Use your defined strategy to help you determine
what you need to learn.

#4

Resolve

Why is resolve so important, and why would I list it as one of the top eight principles of successful sales? Simple: because you need it. Regardless of how good you are, salespeople's lives are full of peaks and valleys. You can significantly shorten your valleys by mastering two fundamental principles: positive thinking and resolve. Don't give up on your strategy, and don't give up on possible accounts after only a few attempts.

Let's talk about resolve. I'll tell you what it means to me: resolve is a consistency of purpose and a consistency of execution. If you take the proper time to build your defined strategy, all that you then need is resolve to reach your goals. Conversely, if you do not properly define your strategy, resolve will get you nothing. Remember that I'm writing this material in a specific order because all of the eight principles are linked together. One without the other will not enable you to attain your full potential. Accomplishing only a few of the eight principles will improve your skills and results, but you will be left with untapped abilities.

If you take the time to properly define your strategy and you also have confidence, then you just need resolve to fully hit your maximum potential. Why? Because things tend to go your way on some days, while on other days they don't. On those days where things don't go your way, you need resolve to continue to pursue your target accounts. If you don't have resolve, the hard times will have you heading home, hitting a local pub, or just surfing the Internet instead of working. Resolve allows you to push forward through thick or thin, and that is a large part of what brings in results.

I understand that you need to learn these principles as you sell; obviously, it's not realistic for you to stop selling and then learn my principles. That is why each principle will help you improve as you are selling. Once you finish with all eight principles, you will notice a transformation that comes from putting the whole package together. That is, the transformation comes from learning and understanding all eight principles. This book is written in such a way that even if you only practice some of the principles, you will see positive results.

For example, let's say that you've been able to note negative thoughts and convert them into positive notions (1). You took the time to gain confidence through the development of a defined strategy (2) and are presentation/conversation ready. You also have a good knowledge of your product base and can easily explain the product's benefits and features (3). Okay, good start. Since I have advised you to learn these steps in order, most likely you're starting to see some positive results —either you're getting additional sales or you're seeing new opportunities within your sales funnel or prospect list.

To help make my point, let's also say that good things are happening and you're on top of the world. Then, suddenly, the earth shakes and bad news appears. Maybe a current customer decides to leave or at the last moment you lose a customer bid to a competitor. Regardless, everyone is upset, and you feel depressed and ready to give up.

We all tend to rationalize what's going on with an account when things don't go our way. We say things like "We didn't have a fair shot" or "They already had their minds made up." Basically, we're making excuses for why we failed. Then, our boss decides to pour it on, constantly reminding us that we didn't get the business. This causes a stir, and everyone wants to change and do things differently. We realize that the strategy we developed isn't working, so we decide to pick apart the plan and find any holes to fix.

Do you see the irony in this situation? The salesperson is trying to explain why the sale was lost, the manager is busy changing how the salespeople go after accounts to make his boss happy, and nothing is being done to learn how to actually improve. More importantly, nothing is being done to ensure resolve.

Again, resolve is based on the assumption that you have a solid, defined strategy. When a loss occurs, it's the result of one of two possibilities: (1) a bad strategy, or (2) someone in the market beat you. A bad strategy is possible if you didn't take the time to develop it. (For more on how to develop a successfully defined strategy, go to www.sales-itworks.com.)

If someone beat you in the marketplace, the important part to note is *how* they beat you. I'm referring to the material or information they explained to the customer that varied from what you gave them. Was it price? Was it quality or perception of quality? Was it innovation or lack of innovation? The fact is that if you have to ask these questions, you didn't do your homework and were beaten by a better sales professional. How did he or she beat you? Your competitor most likely did a better job of preparing than you did. Stop getting beat by lack of preparation by following the eight principles.

Sales—It's That Simple

I've been telling you of the importance of being positive. Confidence and resolve allow me to talk through opportunities. If you have a defined strategy that is effective, you will automatically know the answers to the questions above because they were part of the discussion, and you chose to pass on changing your proposal. Refusing to change your proposal is a choice. Regardless of the result, you did all you needed to as a sales individual.

Resolve is a key component for two reasons. First, it keeps you selling through the difficult time of the bid, and second, it keeps your strategy intact if things start to go downhill. Having resolve will allow you to keep growth more consistent and thus earn more money. One definite truth in sales is that if you consistently change your plan, you will get inconsistency in your sales. If you want continued results, have resolve and execute your strategy.

Don't confuse resolve with the inability to change. Change is a choice in life, something we all need to make part of our lives. Change eliminates boredom and forces all of us to grow as people. Understanding the need for change and continuing to change also requires resolve. The importance of change with respect to resolve can be a complicated issue.

We need to view resolve in two separate categories. The first category, which mainly applies to managers, is to stay the course. Don't continually change your big-picture direction or strategy. Instead, keep it consistent until you really need to change it. Have the patience to believe in your strategy and let it be executed. The second category of resolve is change, and that applies to anyone who sells at any time. You have to be able to change along with your customers and address their specific needs rather than what you want to tell them.

Remember, we all think differently. Since none of us thinks the same, you cannot present the same ideas or thoughts to everyone. Maybe in a corporate environment with internal information you can present the same thing and it will be effective. However, in such a setting, everyone is there to learn direction; ultimately, convincing your colleagues is not near as important as convincing a customer to buy your company's product.

By contrast, in a competitive market, you need to be able to adjust your thoughts to help show your customer why your product is different or unique. The most effective way to do that is to relate to buyers and how they think. I will talk more about change in the next chapter, but note that each of the eight sales principles I'm teaching you are bound together, and once fully understood, they will bring you the success you desire.

Many people have asked me when it's time to change a strategy. My answer? You will know when to change your strategy once you have conquered the eight principles. More importantly, you will know the difference between needing to redefine a strategy and needing to change things up and redefine your areas of focus. Most strategies are good, sound strategies. Those by themselves will carry you for a while, but occasionally we all get bored or stuck in the same daily routine and lose that edge. That edge is what brings success, and we can't afford to lose it. If we find ourselves stuck in that daily routine, we need to redefine the areas of focus that tie directly into our previously defined strategy. How do we do this? Change! We all need to change. In the next chapter, we'll talk about your ability to change.

#4 Resolve
Focus Points:

It is important because:
You *need* it.
Peaks and valleys will crush you without it.
It eliminates wasted time and effort.
It keeps you in the office rather than in the pub, on the Internet, or in front of the TV.
It means you have the ability to learn the eight principles in order.
It keeps you from constant change; improvement is good, but change for the sake of change is not.
It allows you to keep selling through difficult times.
It keeps your strategy intact.

#5

Have the Ability to Change

Of course the ability to change is important. As salespeople, we must continue to learn, improve upon our skills, and make the proper preparation. Change is a part of learning and becoming better at what we do. If we stop changing, we most likely stop learning and progressing. Eventually that will catch up with us and produce stagnant results.

The most difficult part of change is knowing what changes to make. What if we choose to change and it results in worse outcomes? Yes, that does happen. To successfully change with positive results, we need to embrace one major concept: self-actualization, which is fully realizing one's potential.

Do you understand yourself? Do you know who you are? If you answered yes to both questions, then what you need to change is easy to identify. Why?

Because the secret to change lies in understanding yourself. As you learn, you need to choose the information that makes sense to you and adjust it to your personality. Never just change to match what a book told you to do. Instead, take the message that you agree with and mold it to fit your own personality and talents.

If you don't agree with a message or a point in a book or seminar, then don't try it. Take only those points that you agree with, and adjust them accordingly. If you don't agree with a message, then subconsciously it will never work. In the back of your mind, you will always remember telling yourself that it wouldn't work.

Let's say that you're in a seminar and you hear something that intrigues you, but you aren't sure if it makes sense. Wait and think it through. Once you're in full agreement or disagreement, then you know how to move forward. Agreement = move forward and adjust what you've heard to your personality. Disagreement = drop it. Remember that we all think differently; various parts of a book or seminar will affect each individual differently. Thus, I'm not telling you what to learn, but rather how to apply what you learn. Application of education is something all humans are challenged with, and this little secret can spring you into a whole new level of sales.

Sales—It's That Simple

A good friend of mine, whom I highly respect, refuses to change his sales method. Does that method work for him? Absolutely, and he is very good at what he does. In fact, this gentleman is the individual who hired me right out of college. He taught me the basic principles of selling and showed me how to apply those fundamentals so that I could succeed at a young age. He was already well ahead of the game and was willing to share his knowledge to help others learn.

However, my friend stopped learning and thus never changed; consequently, he didn't grow beyond his current level of salesmanship. He stopped at a higher sales ability than most, but he did stop learning and progressing. Whether this lack of change was intentional or not, the results were the same. My point is that you cannot stop learning. You have to continue to ask questions, challenge yourself to learn more, and apply new skills to your personality. Whether you are new to sales or in your fifties and stuck in a daily routine, applying the right kind of change to your sales life will improve your results.

In the previous chapter, I talked about the need to redefine your area of focus. By changing your focus, you inherently keep yourself impassioned, thus giving you the concentration you may have lost. Change can be a great and effective feature. However, it is a lost art that, for some reason, all of us are challenged by. Most people would rather not invite change into their lives because it is hard. Yet as you continue to learn how to change, you will notice how effective and simple it really is. The ability to change comes down to one word that can have a major impact on your life: *choice*. The power in the word *choice* comes directly from you and is empowered by what you do with it.

Changing ourselves is also difficult because it's different from what we're used to. How many of us will go to the same restaurant over and over again? How many eat at the same time every day? How many eat the same sandwich more than three days a week? Take the same way to work every day? Get our daily coffee at the same time?

If we fall into this category, does it mean we cannot change? Absolutely not. We all get stuck on a specific path in life, and we repeat that path over and over again. Taking the same route to work every day is completely normal and very common—it's not an issue. However, for personal improvement, taking the same path every day will prevent you from ever learning another option.

To relate this to the field of sales, if you sell the exact same way all the time, you will never learn or understand another option—an option that may be better than how you currently sell today, or an option that might improve your closing rate. In addition, if you don't understand other sales methods, you won't know how to counter an offer or understand why a buyer may be reluctant. Change is a positive element that each one of us has to make a part of our lives. We don't have to change our path to work or eat fewer of our favorite sandwiches; instead, we need to concentrate on raising our skill level and improving our results.

#5 Have the Ability to Change Focus Points:

The secret to change is to **understand yourself**—
your willingness to learn,
your willingness to change.

It is self-evaluation and the willingness to improve.
Overcome redundancy.

Try to change and improve:
Your **attitude**
Your **skill level**
Your **closing technique**
You **presentation methods**
Your **thought processes**
Your **ability to question**

#6

Execute

Now that you have (1) mastered the power to think positively and (2) learned how to define a strategy that will give you complete confidence in yourself and your company. You have already (3) studied your product, including its features and benefits and how they apply to your customers. You have also convinced yourself that your strategy will work, and you are the very definition of (4) resolve. Lastly, you are willing to (5) change and you understand how to change positively. You understand that learning from others is important. Moreover, you know that once you encounter a thought or comment that you agree with, you should apply it to fit your personality. All done, right? Umm, not quite …

It is wonderful that you now understand the first five principles of sales success. Here they are again, just to recap:

- **Think Positively**

- **Form a Defined Strategy**

- **Know Your Product**

- **Resolve**

- **Have the Ability to Change**

Now on to principle 6: execute. Most of us have an inherent want or need to better ourselves, yet we forget to execute or do anything with what we learn. How many times have we been out with friends when someone makes a great point in the middle of the conversation? We think to ourselves, *I've got to try that*. But we never do. Even though we like the idea and take the time to think about it, we often forget to actually *do* anything about it. We've just squandered an opportunity for growth.

We need to take action on what we learn. This is a constant struggle for most of us, and lack of action on the principles we just covered will put you right back where you started before you read this book. Consider this struggle as a bully. This bully will not let you do what you want to do, which really upsets you. Well, it's time to take a swing at that bully and get your life of improvement back. Start to make yourself apply what you've learned. Tell yourself *I will take ac-*

tion, and begin to do this now. Start to implement your positive thinking. Begin to execute and develop your strategy. Learn your products and show your resolve. Take action and begin to change and improve your skills, both mentally and physically. Execute what you have read today, and show the results. This always reminds me of a saying: those who do are too busy doing it to hear the complaints of those who meant to do it.

Nike's old advertising campaign says it best: "Just do it." You don't have to "do" everything at once. Some people can easily begin to make these changes in their lives, while others will constantly struggle to figure out how to implement these simple steps on a daily basis. Now, one thing is for sure: if you don't implement these suggestions, you will continue to get the same results that you've always gotten.

For those who struggle with accepting or making time for change I recommend the following action: make a list of the key points you learn in this book, and every week or month check one item off the list to concentrate on. Work on this single item, and implement it into your daily routine. As you feel confident that you've fully accepted this change into your life, move on to the next item.

Let's assume that these principles are in fact the items that you seek to learn in more detail—that you want to implement these simple principles into your daily routine so that you can grow as a sales representative and achieve greater results. However, you feel overwhelmed and are uncertain where to begin. Simply start the first week with the positive thoughts section; read it and understand it. Then, execute what you've learned by incorporating positive thinking into your daily routine. Once you've accomplished this item, move on to creating a defined strategy, and so on. You get the idea.

I once had a tape of a motivational speaker, Nido Qubein, that I thought was fantastic. Within his speech he said: "inch by inch, life is a cinch." That is truer than we may realize. If we take steps in life an inch at a time, not only do we ensure that they are accomplished, but we also get a deeper understanding of what each part means. We live in a world of instant gratification, and that mentality by itself can hinder us from achieving all that we could.

Instead, we need to take baby steps and slowly change our thinking and abilities in order to improve. Understanding what and why we are changing is just as important as changing. Likewise, how we execute our thoughts will make a big difference in how each of us may benefit.

#6 Execute
Focus Points:

Learning is easy; implementing what you learn is difficult.

Executing your new knowledge is like a bully; face it to overcome it.

Follow the slogan from Nike: "just do it."

Inch by inch, life is a cinch.

Take baby steps.

#7

Ask

Although this is the most basic principle of all sales, it is also the most common error made in the business world today. People will put together impressive presentations, letters, and handouts, but they fail to ask. "Ask what?" you might say. Simple: ask questions, and ask for the sale.

Salespeople do not ask enough questions. Instead, they seem to like to hear themselves talk and continue to talk about things they feel are relevant and important. In a one-hour meeting, I would bet that the sales individual was talking for forty-five to fifty-five minutes. After that meeting, everyone leaves pumped up and asks each other, "So, do you think they liked it?"

This much I can assure you: if you talk more than 50 percent of the time, the meeting is not likely to be a success. The only way it will be a success is if you were lucky enough to guess exactly what the buyer was looking for and your competition missed it. Instead of taking this risk, all salespeople should become accustomed to asking more questions and getting the prospect's opinions during the presentation. Involve the customers. Help them own the presentation based upon their feedback and the importance of their comments. Customer involvement dramatically increases your chances of success, *if* you're willing to listen.

The same principle applies to phone sales. While on the phone, ask questions, listen for the answers, and pay attention to those answers! While at lunch, ask questions. Most people are itching to share their thoughts and opinions, and that's exactly what sales reps want to hear—and it's exactly what we should pay attention to. Ask questions and listen. Those answers will show you the way to the Promised Land.

I find this section particularly interesting because the word *ask* is such a powerful tool, yet it is not used often enough. Asking questions is a lost art. I cannot tell you how many presentations I have sat through, both good and bad, and at the end the most important question of all is not even asked: "Can I have your business?"

Yes, people forget to ask for the sale, more commonly known as the "close." People forget to close.

Sales—It's That Simple

Trust me—if you don't ask for the business, they probably won't give it to you. Have you ever heard the saying "Ask and you shall receive"? This statement is especially true in sales. Develop a closing statement that fits your personality, and always ask for the business.

If you don't ask this question, you will never know what you need to do to get the business. For instance, if you aren't awarded the business, how do you determine why that was? How can you improve? You have nothing to learn from because you don't know why that result occurred. On the other hand, if you ask for the sale, the buyer will *tell* you the next steps. They will tell you what they liked and did not like. They will answer your questions, and those answers will allow you to clarify any misconceptions and reemphasize key points. That closing question or statement can be the reason why you get the business. It will also help you improve in the future. Having a closing question will help you become a more effective and efficient salesperson.

The key points in this section are as follows:

1. Ask questions, and pay attention to the answers. Use those answers to develop your letters and presentations.

2. Have a closing question, and *use it*.

#7 Ask
Focus Points:

The two most overlooked things in sales:
Ask questions.
Ask for the sale.

You must listen to what the buyer tells you.
Use what you learn in ongoing correspondence.

#8

Understand the Differential Theory

In my opinion, the Differential Theory is the most powerful theory to ever hit the sales profession. I developed this theory based upon my own life experience—specifically, what I learned in the workplace. It is the fundamental difference between good and great. We all want to be great, right? Well, if you can grasp and implement this theory in your daily life, you will be amazed with the results. I picked my title, *Sales: It's That Simple*, on purpose. This theory is not easy to fully understand, but it is certainly simple.

Understanding the "Differential Theory" is your first challenge; implementing it will be your second challenge. It is truly a powerful theory, and I hope that you don't overlook the theory itself because it sounds too simple. In essence, it is learning someone's thought process, which allows you to understand the "why" behind their opinions.

Remember how I told you that I would intentionally repeat myself? I have said, over and over again, *we all think differently*. The Differential Theory explains what that statement really means.

Before I begin, I need each of you to open your mind and really evaluate yourself. Be honest and open, and try to look at yourself through another person's eyes. If you're willing to learn and have the ability and the integrity to be honest with yourself, it will be worth it. This theory will change your professional life (and maybe your personal life as well).

As salespeople, we are challenged to create opportunity out of nothing. We have to talk with people we don't know and get those individuals to trust us—all within a short period of time. In the course of trying to persuade an individual, we hear "no" or "not interested" or "I do not have time" or "call back later" over and over and over again. In time, we become conditioned to hearing certain things from our customers. We need the power of positive thinking to overcome thoughts that often turn negative.

Where the Differential Theory comes into play is not with what we *hear*, but rather with what we *say*. We not only are conditioned by what we hear, we also become conditioned by what we say. Let's say that it took you one year to close a very large account. Finally, after many late nights and continued travel, you were able to get that account. Now you have a proven method for success, right? Wrong! What you have is a one-hit wonder. Why is that? It's because of the Differential Theory.

Here is the Differential Theory. None of us in today's society think exactly alike. It doesn't matter what we as salespeople think. Do not be so arrogant to believe that because you think something is important, your prospect also thinks it is important. The truth is that while you and your customers may sometimes fully understand each other, more often than not you cannot fully appreciate what they are looking for. You must understand that it doesn't matter what you think; rather, it only matters what *they* think.

Again, let me make this point: it doesn't matter what you think; it only matters what they think. If you understand what and how they think, you will have an effective sales presentation and you will grow your business faster than ever before. Stop lecturing based on what you think, and start lecturing based on what your customer thinks. Better yet, if you can learn how they think, you can begin to guess what questions will come up and have answers already prepared.

The Differential Theory is what I've been emphasizing throughout this book: *we all think differently*. If you can grasp this concept, you will begin to see how it helps you become an extremely effective sales person. Stop yourself from telling your customers how something should work. Instead, put yourself in their shoes and create your own letter or presentation. There is nothing wrong with including some of your key points. However, the overall point of what you're saying should be based upon what and how they think.

How do you understand what and how they think? Ask questions and listen. That's it. Pay attention to the little details, and ask your customers why they think or feel as they do. If you don't understand, ask them to explain. Understand the "why," and you will begin to master the Differential Theory. *We all think differently*.

The Differential Theory will cause a lot of people to think about what and how they conduct their dealings in sales. Nevertheless, nothing will change if we are all stuck on what we think and never try to understand how others think. One of the most common practices in life is judging someone's character as a person. We may hold an unfavorable opinion about a specific person or dislike someone before ever knowing him or her. This, too, is part of the Differential Theory. Let's dig deeper.

Sales—It's That Simple

My favorite example of this particular type of difference brings me back to my youth. As a child, I had little self-confidence because I grew quickly and was overweight, which left me awkward and clumsy. I had a few friends that were in the same grade as me, and at times we would play together after school. Sometimes my friends' mothers would approach me and ask whether I thought I was a little old to be playing with their children. Not only did those questions leave me embarrassed, but they also shattered the little confidence I had.

Can you blame the mothers? Not at all; they were just trying to protect their children. But the situation is a prime example of believing something just because your eyes tell you it is true. I was a child who had to deal with adults questioning every move I made, just because I was bigger than normal and physically looked to be older than I really was.

Kids are typically good at not caring what someone looks like, and they accept people as they are, without preconceived notions. As children age, however, our society teaches them to judge others based on appearances or other minor differences. These are inherent assumptions that we make as people, and these assumptions can get into our daily thoughts and affect how we live.

There is no room for assumptions in sales—there is room only for what you know and do not know. The most difficult part of this process is recognizing when we are making those assumptions, because they are inadvertently within us. Assumptions have been conditioned into us, and we need to recondition ourselves to catch our assumptions and form them into questions that will help us discover reality. To do this, you must first understand when and where you make assumptions. Unfortunately, many us will never make this step. But for the ones who do, they will launch themselves into the next level and drastically increase their success.

How can you know when you're making assumptions? There is no clear-cut rule that can be derived from the Differential Theory alone. However, I will give you a few ways to catch yourself. As you begin to create a presentation or letter, ask yourself whether you know the answer to a specific question or point you're making, or whether you're just making an assumption. If you determine that it is an assumption, create a list of questions to ask during the next phone conversation with your potential customer. Get your answer, and then get back to work on that presentation or letter.

My experience tells me that some of you will struggle to understand the difference between assumption and fact. In fact, many people have convinced themselves that they're correct in thought and principle, which makes it difficult for them to distinguish between assumption and fact. They don't mean to think this way, yet it is how their minds work. For those individuals, take the time to reflect on what you did and why you did it. It's okay to assume something as long as you're aware that you're doing it. Earlier I mentioned that there is no room for assumptions in sales. Let me clarify: there is no room for assumptions believed to be facts in sales. We're all going to have assumptions. Bad assumptions are only those assumptions that you are not aware of. It is okay to make assumptions—but not when you believe them to be reality.

By now, I hope that you've begun to understand that everything I'm teaching you is to help you to more effectively prepare, which will increase your rate of success. Some people may ask, "If I don't believe in it, why should I sell it?" My answer: if you don't believe in what you sell, move on. Don't sell products that you don't believe in. There are so many great products and companies today; don't let yourself get caught in a negative situation, as that will take you down a road that will be difficult to overcome.

Other people ask, "Why do you want to understand how and why prospects or clients think? Isn't that manipulative?" The reason you want to understand the how and why is to better relate to your buyer. I'm assuming that everyone has a great product. Once you understand how to relate to the buyer, you can help him or her by better explaining why your product is superior. That helps set the sale in motion and thus increases your odds.

#8 Understand the Differential Theory Focus Points:

We all think differently.
The theory is the realization that it doesn't matter what we think, only what our customer thinks.

To Apply It
Learn to understand how and why your customers think that way.
You don't have to agree with them—just understand them.
You don't have to convince them you're right
(… yet) —just understand why
they think that way.

The Secret
Know whether something is a fact or you've made an assumption.
It may be a fact for you, but it might be an assumption that the customer agrees with you.

Conclusion

Sales: It's That Simple was written to help each of you become better within the field of sales. You can only improve and become great at what you do for a living by taking the time needed to learn each principle. It is not an easy undertaking, but it *is* very simple. Take the time to learn each principle and truly make them part of your daily selling experience.

These principles are the foundation for your success. I understand that there may be questions that need to be answered, and I understand that you may have doubts. That is why I created my website: www.sales-itworks.com. This website was constructed to help give you further guidance and encouragement as you implement these principles into your daily life. The best advice I can give you is to just get started. Jump in, take action, and start your journey to a brand-new life within the field of sales. If you learn and implement my principles into your life, I believe they will jump-start your attitude and your career. It will bring focus in times of confusion. It will bring you options when all your co-workers are out of options. It will bring you business when others are unable to bring in business. It will bring you clarity for today and for tomorrow. I believe that my principles will ultimately bring more sales than ever before. This book teaches you the reasons behind making good decisions, and that is exactly what these principles will force you to do. Good luck, and I wish each of you great success in the future.

The 8 Simple Principles of Sales:

1. Think Positively

2. Form a Defined Strategy

3. Know Your Product

4. Resolve

5. Have the Ability to Change

6. Execute

7. Ask

8. Understand the Differential Theory

If you are interested in having Dave speak at your next sales meeting or event, please contact him via his website: www.sales-itworks.com.

www.ingramcontent.com/pod-product-compliance
Lightning Source LLC
Chambersburg PA
CBHW030913180526
45163CB00004B/1820